GRAPHIC BATTLES OF WORLD WAR II ™

THE BATTLE OF
IWO JIMA

GUERRILLA WARFARE IN THE PACIFIC

By **Larry Hama** Illustrated by **Anthony Williams**

rosen publishing's
rosen central

New York

Published in 2007 by The Rosen Publishing Group, Inc.
29 East 21st Street, New York, NY 10010

Copyright © 2007 Rosen Book Works, LLC, New York, NY, and Osprey Publishing Ltd, Oxford, England

First edition, 2007

Photo Credits: p. 4 Courtesy of the Boeing Company Archives; p. 5 (top and bottom) National Archives and Records Administration; p. 7 National Archives and Records Administration; p. 44 U.S. Navy; p. 45 (top and bottom) National Archives and Records Administration

Simone Drinkwater, Series Editor, Osprey Publishing
Nel Yomtov, Series Editor, Rosen Book Works

Library of Congress Cataloging-in-Publication Data

Hama, Larry.
    The battle of Iwo Jima: guerrilla warfare in the Pacific / by Larry Hama.—
    1st ed.
    p. cm. – (Graphic battles of World War II)
    Includes bibliographical references and index.
    ISBN-13 978-1-4042-0781-3 (lib.)   978-1-4042-6030-6 (pbk.)
    ISBN-10 1-4042-0781-3 (lib.)   1-4042-6030-7 (pbk.)
    6-pack ISBN-13 978-1-4042-7421-1   6-pack ISBN-10 1-4042-7421-9
    1. Iwo Jima, Battle of, Japan, 1945–Juvenile literature. I. Title. II. Series.

D767.99.I9H35 2007
940.54'2528–dc22

                         2006007645

CONTENTS

WORLD WAR II, 1939–1945

Following World War I (1914–1918), hostilities remained among many countries. To avoid more fighting, the United States tried to build good relations with other nations and to stay out of their affairs.

In Asia, Japan was becoming aggressive toward its neighbors, especially China. In Europe, Italy invaded Ethiopia in 1936. Germany, under Adolf Hitler, took control of Austria and Czechoslovakia in 1938.

Germany then invaded Poland. France and England declared war on Germany. Still, America avoided serious involvement in the widening conflict. On December 7, 1941, Japan attacked the U.S. naval base at Pearl Harbor, Hawaii. The next day, America declared war on Japan. Then Germany declared war on America.

For the next four years, U.S. forces fought Japan in the Pacific Ocean. To get closer to the Japanese mainland, the United States had to conquer one small Pacific island after another. One of the bloodiest battles was fought on Iwo Jima, a deadly 5-mile-wide stretch of volcanic ash.

KEY COMMANDERS

Lt. General Tadamichi Kuribayashi
Led Japanese troops against China, fought against Russia, and commanded the Imperial Guard. Japanese emperor Hirohito chose him to defend Iwo Jima.

Lt. Colonel Baron Taeichi Nishi
Commanded a tank regiment at Iwo Jima. It is believed he committed suicide when he thought the Americans would win the battle.

Admiral Raymond Spruance
In 1942, he was in command at the Battle of Midway, where he won the most important victory of the Pacific war.

General Holland M. ("Howling Mad") Smith
Developed many tactics that made success in the Pacific war possible. Although an administrator, he went to Iwo Jima, giving support to U.S. forces.

STOPPING THE JAPANESE WAR MACHINE

In 1941, Japan's military dictatorship went to war with the United States. Their goal was to obtain resources, mainly oil, for their war against China. But even by 1945, after several years of bitter and brutal fighting in the Pacific against the Americans, Japan's industries at home remained untouched and in full production. The United States and its allies had to find a way to stop Japan's production abilities without having to invade the island—a move that could have cost hundreds of thousands of Allied lives.

Taking on that challenge, the United States developed a way to reach the Japanese islands and destroy its ability to build weapons and other war materiel. That development was the Boeing B-29 Superfortress bomber.

Work on the plane had actually begun in 1938. The Superfortress had a flying range of over 5,000 miles. It was rushed into production, but it had many problems, especially with its engines. Nevertheless, 150 of the giant bombers began operations in June 1944. Flying from air bases in India, the giant planes flew to China, refueled, and then bombed Japan from high altitudes. However, the results were poor. There was tremendous loss of both planes and airmen, due mostly to mechanical problems in the bombers.

Still, the Allied forces continued to tighten the noose around the Japanese mainland. In June and July 1944, American forces seized the Marianas Islands of Guam, Saipan, and Tinian. Flying from runways

The Boeing B-29 Superfortress bomber was the most advanced aircraft of its time. It was the first Allied plane that was able to reach Japan easily.

on these islands, the B-29s were now much closer to Japan. Prince Higashikuni, Commander of Home Defense Headquarters, later admitted, "The war was lost when the Marianas were taken." Prime Minister Hideki Tojo, under pressure from Emperor Hirohito, resigned on July 9, 1944. But the war went on.

Thoughts on both sides turned to the tiny island of Iwo Jima. The island is in the Bonin-Volcano Islands group, halfway between the Marianas and Japan. Iwo Jima was only eight square miles. It had two airfields with a third under construction. The Japanese used it as a naval base and as a radar warning station. If the Americans could take control of the island, the airfields could be used by U.S. fighter planes to safely escort the B-29s back to their bases in the Marianas. At the urging of Admiral Raymond Spruance, the Americans decided to launch an invasion of this important piece of land.

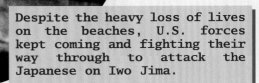

Despite the heavy loss of lives on the beaches, U.S. forces kept coming and fighting their way through to attack the Japanese on Iwo Jima.

"The fighting was the toughest the Marines ran across in one hundred and sixty-eight years."

–U.S. general "Howling Mad" Smith

In spring 1944, Lt. Gen. Tadamichi Kuribayashi was appointed Iwo Jima's commander. He had a mixture of 5,000 army and naval personnel to defend the island. Kuribayashi immediately asked his superiors for more troops, artillery, and construction materials. Oddly enough, Kuribayashi's request was actually helped by the American victories in the Marianas. Soon, Japanese army troops and naval infantry, once intended for the now-captured

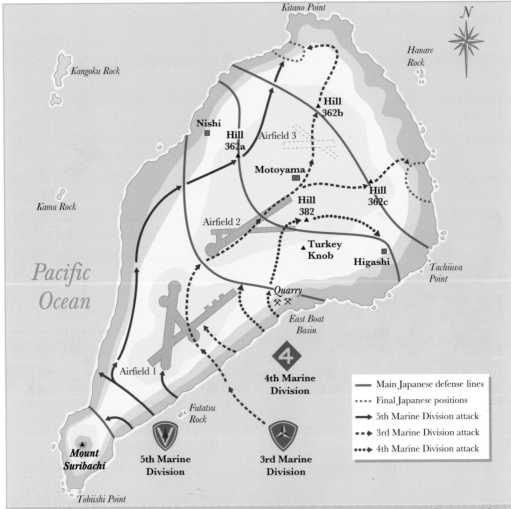

U.S. Marines of the 3rd, 4th, and 5th Divisions invaded Iwo Jima on February 19, 1945. In a bitter fight, the Marines were able to push back and overcome the Japanese, cornering them on the edges of the island. The fierce battle lasted thirty-six days.

Flamethrowers helped clear the many caves and underground tunnels on Iwo Jima where the Japanese were hiding.

Marianas, began to arrive. Eventually, about 23,000 Japanese troops were on the island, preparing for an attack by the Americans.

In earlier landing attacks by U.S. forces on Japanese-held islands, the Japanese had used their standard tactics of defeating the enemy. However, facing enormous American firepower, these had little success, nor did the other tactic of a counterattack at full force. This kind of counterattack was a "banzai charge," a suicidal infantry attack in which no one expects to survive.

To defeat the U.S. forces on Iwo Jima, Kuribayashi had another idea. He ordered his men to dig in, even dig in their tanks. Hundreds of pillboxes, or concrete defense points, and firing positions were built. The island's natural caves were enlarged. These were connected by a system of underground tunnels. Large minefields were also made to defend against the Americans. Kuribayashi forbade any banzai attacks. His men would let the Americans come to them. Each man took a vow to kill ten Americans before he died.

To capture Iwo Jima, the United States would use the three Marine Divisions of Major General Harry Schmidt's V Amphibious Corps, over 70,000 troops. They would be supported by a naval fleet commanded by Admiral Spruance. In preparation, a bombing campaign against the island was ordered. Other than destroying the Japanese planes on the island, it proved ineffective.

The Iwo Jima invasion, called Operation Detachment, had to be done quickly between the January 9 invasion of Luzon, Philippines, and the April 1 invasion of Okinawa. Iwo Jima's operation was expected to take four to five days.

The Marines had wanted nine days of preinvasion naval bombardment. But Spruance was worried about the threat of kamikaze suicide plane attacks. He allowed only three days, with only part of his fleet. As the invasion began, his main force would attack airfields in Japan.

Preinvasion bombardment began on February 16, amid cold and rainy weather. One day of bombardment was cancelled. On the morning of February 19, 1945, the American landing craft went in.

7

THE BATTLE OF IWO JIMA
GUERRILLA WARFARE IN THE PACIFIC

ON THE MORNING OF FEBRUARY 19, 1945, THREE U.S. MARINE DIVISIONS OF OVER 70,000 MEN MADE AN AMPHIBIOUS ATTACK ON THE JAPANESE-HELD ISLAND OF IWO JIMA.

A LARGE FLEET OF BATTLESHIPS, CRUISERS, AND DESTROYERS HAD FIRED AT THE ISLAND FOR THREE DAYS TO PREPARE FOR THE LANDING.

PLANES BASED ON AIRCRAFT CARRIERS FLEW HUNDREDS OF BOMBING MISSIONS. JAPANESE AIR OPPOSITION WAS A SINGLE ZERO FIGHTER.

IT WAS QUICKLY SHOT DOWN BY AN OBSERVATION FLOATPLANE FROM THE USS PENSACOLA.

THE FIRST WAVE OF AMPHIBIOUS MARINE FIGHTING VEHICLES DROVE ONTO THE SOUTH SHORE OF IWO JIMA. IT MET LITTLE RESISTANCE...

... BUT WAS STOPPED DEAD BY 15-FOOT-HIGH TERRACES OF SOFT BLACK VOLCANIC ASH.

TANKS AND LANDING VEHICLES GOT STUCK AND COULD NOT MOVE.

THE TROOPS SANK TO THEIR ANKLES. EVERY STEP WAS A MAJOR EFFORT.

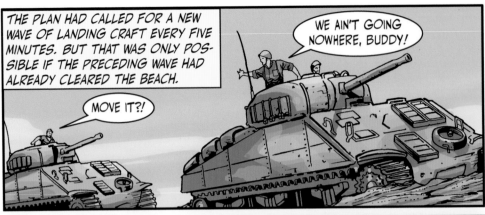

THE PLAN HAD CALLED FOR A NEW WAVE OF LANDING CRAFT EVERY FIVE MINUTES. BUT THAT WAS ONLY POSSIBLE IF THE PRECEDING WAVE HAD ALREADY CLEARED THE BEACH.

WE AIN'T GOING NOWHERE, BUDDY!

MOVE IT?!

THE TIDE CAME FROM THE SIDE. IT MADE STEERING HARD AND SWAMPED SOME BOATS.

THE LANDING BEACHES BECAME CROWDED WITH STUCK AND DISABLED BOATS AND VEHICLES.

MARINES DROPPED THEIR HEAVY PACKS AND KEPT ONLY THEIR WEAPONS AND AMMUNITION.

I MIGHT NEED THIS LATER...

YOU FIGURE ON LIVING THAT LONG?

THIS IS TOO EASY, SIR! THE JAPANESE SHOULD HAVE HAD ARTILLERY ZEROED IN ON EVERY INCH OF THIS BEACH—

IT JUST GOES TO SHOW HOW EFFECTIVE OUR NAVAL BOMBARDMENT WAS.

U.S. ADMIRAL CHESTER NIMITZ WAS COMMANDER IN CHIEF PACIFIC (CINCPAC). HE HAD NEVER LOST A SEA BATTLE.

IN OCTOBER 1944, THE JOINT CHIEFS OF STAFF HAD ORDERED HIM TO OCCUPY IWO JIMA.

ADMIRAL NIMITZ ENTRUSTED THE PLANNING AND ORGANIZATION OF THIS OPERATION TO THREE TACTICAL MASTERMINDS.

THE FIRST WAS ADMIRAL RAYMOND A. SPRUANCE, THE INTELLIGENT OPERATIONS COMMANDER.

SECOND WAS ADMIRAL RICHMOND K. TURNER, A GENIUS AT ORGANIZATION. HE WAS THE JOINT EXPEDITIONARY FORCE COMMANDER.

THIRD WAS LIEUTENANT GENERAL HOLLAND M. SMITH, KNOWN AS "HOWLING MAD" BY THE MARINES HE COMMANDED. HE WAS COMMANDING GENERAL MARINE FORCE PACIFIC.

BUT WHEN THE MARINES HIT THE BEACH, IT WAS MAJOR GENERAL HARRY "THE DUTCHMAN" SCHMIDT, COMMANDER OF V AMPHIBIOUS CORPS, WHO WAS GIVING THE ORDERS THAT MATTERED.

11

BY AUGUST 1944, U.S. FORCES HAD TAKEN THE ISLANDS OF GUAM, SAIPAN, AND TINIAN, IN THE MARIANAS.

FROM THE ISLANDS, U.S. FORCES LAUNCHED BOMBING RAIDS ON JAPANESE CITIES AND INDUSTRIAL SITES WITH THE BIG, LONG-RANGE* B-29 SUPERFORTRESS BOMBERS.

SCRATCH ONE BALL BEARING FACTORY OFF YOUR LIST!

*IT WAS 1,580 MILES ONE WAY FROM GUAM TO TOKYO.

IWO JIMA WAS ABOUT HALFWAY BETWEEN THE MARIANAS AND TOKYO. THE JAPANESE HAD TWO AIRFIELDS ON THE ISLAND THAT COULD LAUNCH FIGHTERS CAPABLE OF SHOOTING DOWN THE B-29S.

THERE WAS ALSO A RADAR STATION THAT COULD WARN TOKYO OF AN INCOMING ATTACK. IWO JIMA HAD TO BE TAKEN.

MAYDAY! I'M GOING DOWN!

THERE ARE NO AIR-SEA RESCUE FLYING BOATS IN RANGE--SORRY.

IWO JIMA COULD ALSO SERVE AS AN EMERGENCY LANDING STRIP FOR CRIPPLED U.S. BOMBERS AND AS A BASE FOR LONG-RANGE FIGHTER ESCORTS.

THE JAPANESE COMMANDER OF IWO JIMA WAS LIEUTENANT GENERAL TADAMICHI KURIBAYASHI.

HE CAME FROM A SAMURAI FAMILY AND HAD GIVEN THIRTY YEARS OF EXCELLENT SERVICE TO THE ARMY.

KURIBAYASHI HAD SPENT TIME IN THE UNITED STATES AS A MINOR DIPLOMAT WHERE HE GREW TO LIKE AND ADMIRE AMERICANS.

HE WROTE TO HIS FAMILY, "THE UNITED STATES IS THE LAST COUNTRY IN THE WORLD THAT JAPAN SHOULD FIGHT."

BUT HE HAD BEEN GIVEN THE JOB OF DEFENDING IWO JIMA -- TO THE LAST MAN IF NECESSARY.

IN A LETTER TO HIS WIFE, HE SAID, "DO NOT PLAN FOR MY RETURN."

JAPANESE ARTILLERY WAS DUG IN AND WELL HIDDEN. THEY HAD BEEN HOLDING THEIR FIRE, WAITING FOR THE MARINES TO MOVE OFF THE BEACHES...

... BUT THE MASS OF TROOPS AT THE SHORE-LINE WAS TOO PERFECT A TARGET TO PASS UP.

I TOLD YOU WE WERE IN FOR IT!

STEWARD'S MATE CLEVELAND WASHINGTON, A SEABEE,* KNEELED TO PRAY.

*NAVY CONSTRUCTION BATTALION ENGINEERS (CBs) WERE ON THE BEACH FROM THE START. THEY CLEARED PATHS FOR THE TANKS.

YOU SEABEES! GET UP ON THAT TERRACE!

WASHINGTON WAS UNTRAINED IN WEAPONS. HE SPENT THE NEXT THREE DAYS IN THE THICK OF THE BATTLE, AS AN AMMUNITION BEARER.

GENERAL KURIBAYASHI KNEW THAT HE HAD NO HOPE OF WINNING. HIS PLAN WAS TO INFLICT AS MANY CASUALTIES AS HE COULD ON THE AMERICANS.

TO DO THIS, KURIBAYASHI HAD, IN NINE MONTHS, TURNED MUCH OF THE ISLAND INTO A COMPLEX OF FORTIFICATIONS.

THERE WERE MACHINE GUN NESTS, CAVES, GUN EMPLACEMENTS, PILLBOXES, AND COMMAND POSTS.

THEY WERE ALL LINKED BY A LARGE SYSTEM OF TUNNELS. SOME RAN 75 FEET DEEP.

IT WAS POSSIBLE TO TRAVEL FOUR MILES COMPLETELY UNDERGROUND.

THE CONCRETE BLOCKHOUSES WERE STRONG ENOUGH TO WITHSTAND WEEKS OF NAVAL SHELLING AND AERIAL BOMBING.

SOMEHOW, IN THE MIDDLE OF THIS, A GROUP OF YOUNG JAPANESE BOTANY STUDENTS HAD ARRIVED AT IWO JIMA ON A SCHOOL FIELD TRIP.

WITH NO WAY OF GETTING OFF THE ISLAND, EACH STUDENT WAS GIVEN TWO HAND GRENADES -- ONE FOR THE ENEMY, ONE FOR HIMSELF.

BY 10:30 A.M. ON FEBRUARY 19, PARTS OF THE MARINES 23RD REGIMENT HAD MOVED PAST THE TERRACES. THEY WERE ADVANCING TOWARD AIRFIELD 1 THROUGH INTENSE MACHINE-GUN FIRE.

THEY WERE MET BY WHAT SEEMED TO BE A SOLID WALL OF BLOCKHOUSES AND PILLBOXES.

COVER ME!

WHO WAS THAT?

THAT WAS SGT. COLE, SIR.

SERGEANT DARREN COLE, ARMED ONLY WITH A PISTOL AND GRENADES, SINGLE-HANDEDLY SILENCED FIVE PILLBOXES FILLED WITH JAPANESE TROOPS.

COLE WAS KILLED BY A GRENADE, BUT HE HAD OPENED A PASSAGE FOR HIS FELLOW MARINES.

FEBRUARY 20. BY THE END OF THE SECOND DAY OF THE INVASION, D+1*, THE MARINES HAD TAKEN MOST OF IWO JIMA'S AIRFIELD 1.

*DAY ONE PLUS 1, THE ARMY REFERS TO THIS AS D+1.

AT DUSK ON FEBRUARY 21, D+2, A FLIGHT OF 50 JAPANESE PLANES, MOSTLY ZERO FIGHTERS, ATTACKED THE NAVY SHIPS SUPPORTING THE INVASION.

IT WAS ONE OF THE EARLY KAMIKAZE* ATTACKS OF THE WAR.

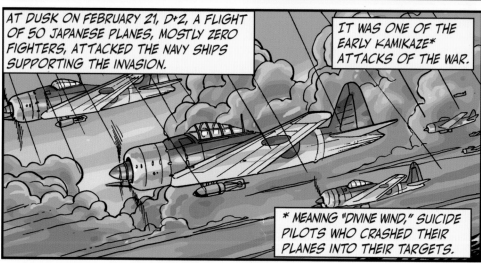

* MEANING "DIVINE WIND," SUICIDE PILOTS WHO CRASHED THEIR PLANES INTO THEIR TARGETS.

THE CARRIER SARATOGA WAS SEVERELY DAMAGED. THE ESCORT CARRIER BISMARCK SEA WAS SUNK AND 341 MEN WERE KILLED IN THE ATTACK.

BY THE END OF FEBRUARY 22, D+3, GENERAL "HOWLING MAD" SMITH ABOARD THE USS *AUBURN* HAD BEEN TOLD THAT MARINE CASUALTIES WERE 4,574 DEAD AND WOUNDED.

HE HAD TOLD REPORTERS THAT THE MARINES WOULD TAKE IWO JIMA NO MATTER WHAT THE COST. IT WAS A COMMENT THAT HE WOULD PAY DEARLY FOR.

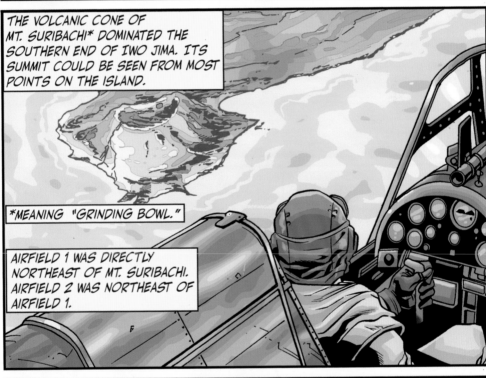

THE VOLCANIC CONE OF MT. SURIBACHI* DOMINATED THE SOUTHERN END OF IWO JIMA. ITS SUMMIT COULD BE SEEN FROM MOST POINTS ON THE ISLAND.

*MEANING "GRINDING BOWL."

AIRFIELD 1 WAS DIRECTLY NORTHEAST OF MT. SURIBACHI. AIRFIELD 2 WAS NORTHEAST OF AIRFIELD 1.

GENERAL KURIBAYASHI HAD EXPECTED HIS UNITS THAT WERE DUG INTO MT. SURIBACHI TO HOLD THE MARINES FOR AT LEAST A WEEK.

BUT AFTER THREE DAYS OF NAVAL SHELLING AND CONSTANT MARINE ASSAULTS, MOST OF THE JAPANESE SURVIVORS FLED.

THE REMAINING JAPANESE MADE THE AMERICANS PAY FOR EVERY INCH OF MT. SURIBACHI IN BLOOD.

ON FEBRUARY 23, D+4, AT 10:20 A.M., A PATROL FROM THE 28TH REGIMENT TOOK THE SUMMIT AND RAISED THE STARS AND STRIPES.

MARINES ALL OVER THE SOUTHERN END OF IWO JIMA CHEERED.

THE FLAG IS UP!

JAPANESE TROOPS COULD SEE IT AS WELL.

HEN-NA MONO DA.*

*"THIS IS A VERY BAD THING."

AT 12:00 P.M., CAMERAMAN JOE ROSENTHAL TOOK THE MOST FAMOUS PHOTO OF THE WAR AS A SECOND, LARGER FLAG WAS RAISED TO REPLACE THE FIRST FLAG.

OF THE SIX MARINES WHO RAISED THE SECOND FLAG, ONLY THREE SURVIVED THE BATTLE.

ONE OF THE SURVIVORS WAS IRA HAYES, A NATIVE AMERICAN OF THE PIMA TRIBE FROM ARIZONA.

A TRIBAL ELDER HAD TOLD HAYES WHAT IT MEANT TO BE AN HONORABLE WARRIOR.

FIGHT BRAVELY. KILL IF YOU MUST, BUT TAKE NO PRIDE IN IT. IF YOU RETURN, WE WILL KNOW YOUR DEEDS. NEVER BOAST OF WHAT YOU DID IN WAR.

THE FLAG-RAISING PHOTO MADE IRA HAYES A NATIONAL HERO. HE WAS SENT AROUND THE COUNTRY ON A TOUR TO SELL WAR BONDS.

HE WASN'T BOASTING HIMSELF, BUT IT WAS ALL THE SAME TO HIS TRIBE. HE HAD BROKEN ONE OF ITS MAJOR TABOOS.

21

ON THE DAY THE FLAG WENT UP, GENERAL HARRY SCHMIDT CAME ASHORE TO SET UP HIS HEADQUARTERS.

IT'S THE DUTCHMAN HIMSELF!

LOOKS SALTIER IN PERSON, DON'T HE?

BY FEBRUARY 25, D+6, AIRFIELD 1 WAS SWARMING WITH 2,000 SEABEES. THEY WERE EXTENDING THE RUNWAYS SO THEY COULD LAND THE B-29 BOMBERS.

THE AIRFIELD WAS STILL WELL WITHIN RANGE OF ENEMY ARTILLERY, BUT THIS DID NOT STOP THE SEABEES.

NOR DID THE DEADLY FIRE FROM JAPANESE SNIPERS.

THE 133RD NAVY CONSTRUCTION BATTALION LANDED ON IWO JIMA WITH THE SECOND WAVE ON DAY ONE. THEY SUFFERED 245 CASUALTIES, THE HIGHEST OF ANY SEABEE UNIT IN HISTORY.

22

NAVY CORPSMEN WERE THE EQUIVALENT OF ARMY MEDICS FOR THE MARINES. THEY WERE IN THE THICK OF THE FIGHTING, TENDING TO THE WOUNDED, AND TOOK SEVERE CASUALTIES THEMSELVES.

PHARMACIST'S MATE 2ND CLASS GEORGE E. WAHLEN HAD ALREADY BEEN WOUNDED TWICE. HE REFUSED TO EVACUATE SO HE COULD CONTINUE TO TREAT HIS COMRADES.

23 DOCTORS AND 827 CORPSMEN WERE KILLED OR WOUNDED ON IWO JIMA.

WOUNDED A THIRD TIME AND UNABLE TO WALK, WAHLEN DRAGGED HIMSELF BY HIS HANDS ALONG THE GROUND FOR 50 YARDS TO AID A FALLEN MARINE.

PA14·9

WHEN HE WAS FINALLY EVACUATED, WAHLEN HAD BEEN DOING HIS JOB NONSTOP FOR FIVE DAYS AND NIGHTS.

THE FLAMETHROWER WAS ONE OF THE MOST DESTRUCTIVE WEAPONS USED BY THE MARINES ON IWO JIMA.

IT USED COMPRESSED GAS TO THROW A FLAMING MIXTURE OF OIL-BASED FUEL AND ALUMINUM UP TO FIFTY YARDS.

DURING THE FIGHT FOR AIRFIELD 2, THE 1ST BATTALION OF THE 21ST REGIMENT, 3RD DIVISION, RAN INTO A COMPLEX OF BUNKERS AND ANTITANK EMPLACEMENTS.

WILLIAMS, FRONT AND CENTER!

CORPORAL HERSHEL "WOODY" WILLIAMS WAS THE LAST FLAME-THROWER MAN LEFT.

ESCORTED BY A SMALL TEAM OF RIFLEMEN, WILLIAMS BURNED OUT BUNKER AFTER BUNKER IN THE FACE OF INTENSE RIFLE AND MACHINE-GUN FIRE.

ON ONE BUNKER, HE CREPT UP ON TOP AND INSERTED THE NOZZLE OF HIS FLAMETHROWER THROUGH THE AIR VENT.

AT ONE POINT, HE EVEN STOPPED A BAYONET CHARGE.

AFTER FOUR HOURS, WILLIAMS HAD SUCCEEDED IN CLEARING A PATH THROUGH THE BUNKER COMPLEX.

24

AS THE MARINES ADVANCED NORTH-EAST FROM AIRFIELD 2, THEY ENCOUNTERED A GROUP OF JAPANESE DEFENSIVE POSITIONS THAT WAS TO BE KNOWN FROM THEN ON AS "THE MEATGRINDER."

THE JAPANESE HELD THE HIGH GROUND ON HILL 382 AND "THE TURKEY KNOB."*

FIGHTING WAS UPHILL ALL THE WAY, ON GROUND COVERED WITH BOULDERS AND STEEP GULLIES.

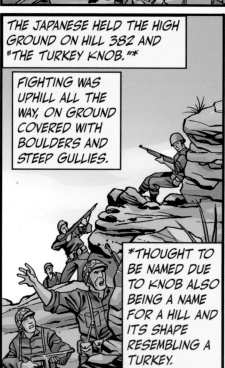

*THOUGHT TO BE NAMED DUE TO KNOB ALSO BEING A NAME FOR A HILL AND ITS SHAPE RESEMBLING A TURKEY.

SHERMAN TANKS FITTED WITH BULLDOZER BLADES TRIED UNSUCCESSFULLY TO CLEAR PATHS FOR BATTLE TANKS AND OTHER VEHICLES.

AT NIGHT, THE JAPANESE TRIED TO RESUPPLY THEIR GARRISON BY PARACHUTE AIRDROPS. VERY LITTLE GOT THROUGH, AND THREE PLANES WERE SHOT DOWN.

THE 23RD MARINES MADE THEIR WAY THROUGH A MINEFIELD AT THE BASE OF HILL 382.

ONE OF THEM WAS PFC (PRIVATE FIRST CLASS) DOUGLAS T. JACOBSON.

JACOBSON WAS A 19-YEAR-OLD RESERVIST FROM PORT WASHINGTON, NEW YORK. HE PICKED UP A BAZOOKA FROM A FALLEN COMRADE...

... AND ATTACKED BLOCKHOUSES AND GUN EMPLACEMENTS BY HIMSELF.

LOADING AND FIRING A ROCKET LAUNCHER IS A TWO-MAN OPERATION. SOMEHOW, JACOBSON MANAGED IT ALONE.

PFC JACOBSON KNOCKED OUT SIXTEEN EMPLACEMENTS AND KILLED 75 ENEMY SOLDIERS.

ROCKET-LAUNCHING TRUCKS WERE ALSO PART OF THE ASSAULT ON HILL 382. THEY FIRED MORE THAN 500 MISSILES.

MARINE ARTILLERY BATTERIES KEPT UP A CONSTANT SHELLING. THEY WERE SOAKING ENEMY AREAS WITH HIGH EXPLOSIVES.

WHERE TANKS COULD CROSS THE ROUGH GROUND, THEY DID THEIR SHARE.

BUT NOTHING SEEMED TO DO ANY GOOD IN LESSENING THE STEADILY MOUNTING TOLL OF U.S. DEAD AND WOUNDED.

A LARGE PERCENTAGE OF THE MARINES WHO MADE THE FIRST LANDING AT IWO JIMA WERE VETERANS OF PREVIOUS BATTLES IN THE PACIFIC.

BUT THE BATTLE REPLACEMENTS THAT WERE SENT IN TO FILL THE THINNING RANKS HAD LITTLE FIGHTING EXPERIENCE.

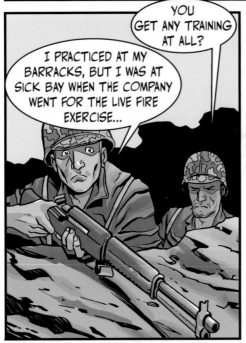

YOU GET ANY TRAINING AT ALL?

I PRACTICED AT MY BARRACKS, BUT I WAS AT SICK BAY WHEN THE COMPANY WENT FOR THE LIVE FIRE EXERCISE...

WHAT'S THAT WEIRD SOUND? LIKE BEES, OR--

THOSE ARE BULLETS, BOY--

MAJOR GENERAL ERSKINE, COMMANDER OF THE 3RD MARINE DIVISION, SAID OF THE REPLACEMENTS, "THEY GET KILLED THE DAY BEFORE THEY GO INTO BATTLE."

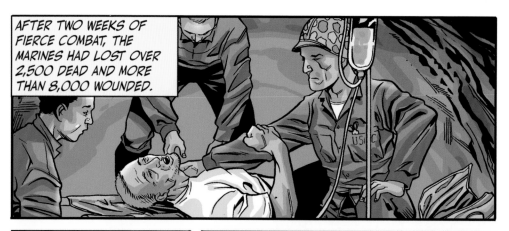

AFTER TWO WEEKS OF FIERCE COMBAT, THE MARINES HAD LOST OVER 2,500 DEAD AND MORE THAN 8,000 WOUNDED.

THE BATTLE HAD DRAGGED ON LONGER THAN THE CHIEFS OF STAFF HAD EXPECTED.

DURING THE FIERCE FIGHTING AT TARAWA, THE U.S. NEARLY RAN OUT OF MEN. NOW, GENERAL SMITH'S STAFF REMEMBERED THAT HE HAD ORDERED THEM TO FIGHT AT TARAWA UNDER HIS COMMAND.

IT TURNED OUT THEY DIDN'T HAVE TO GO. BUT THE SITUATION ON IWO JIMA WAS STARTING TO LOOK THE SAME.

GENERAL KURIBAYASHI RADIOED A MESSAGE TO TOKYO.

... OUR STRONGPOINTS MIGHT BE ABLE TO FIGHT, DELAYING ACTIONS FOR SEVERAL MORE DAYS. MY OFFICERS AND MEN DIE WITHOUT REGRET...*

*TRANSLATED FROM JAPANESE.

IN FACT, THE JAPANESE GARRISON HELD OUT FOR THREE MORE WEEKS.

ON MARCH 4, D+13, "DINAH MIGHT," A BADLY DAMAGED B-29 RETURNING FROM A BOMBING RAID SOUTHWEST OF TOKYO, REQUESTED AN EMERGENCY LANDING.

AS THE PLANE SET DOWN ON AIRFIELD 1, JAPANESE ARTILLERY ZEROED IN ON THE RUNWAY.

THE PILOT TAXIED CLEAR WITHOUT GETTING HIT.

IWO JIMA HAD NOT EVEN BEEN COMPLETELY TAKEN YET AND ALREADY ITS AIRFIELDS WERE SAVING THE LIVES OF AMERICAN BOMBER CREWS.

ON MARCH 6, D+15, COMBINED NAVY AND MARINE ARTILLERY FIRED 23,000 ROUNDS IN A SINGLE 67-MINUTE BARRAGE.

DIVE-BOMBERS FROM U.S. CARRIERS POUNDED THE ENEMY POSITIONS WITH HIGH EXPLOSIVES AND NAPALM CANISTERS. *

*JELLIED GASOLINE THAT BURSTS INTO FLAME ON IMPACT.

"ZIPPO" FLAMETHROWING SHERMAN TANKS LED THE WAY, BURNING EVERYTHING IN THEIR PATH.

BUT JAPANESE RESISTANCE WAS JUST AS FIERCE AS EVER.

MARINE DAVID WORLEY WROTE, "THERE ARE BODIES EVERYWHERE. THE GROUND IS SPOTTED WITH BLOOD..."

ON MARCH 7, D+16, A BATTALION COMMANDED BY LT. COL. CUSHMAN WAS ADVANCING ON HILL 362C WHEN IT GOT SURROUNDED BY A JAPANESE TANK REGIMENT FIGHTING ON FOOT.*

*THE JAPANESE HAD NO TANKS LEFT AND FOUGHT AS INFANTRY.

THE REGIMENT WAS LED BY LIEUTENANT COLONEL (BARON) NISHI, A WEALTHY ARISTOCRAT WITH FAMILY TIES TO THE JAPANESE EMPEROR.

BARON NISHI HAD WON A GOLD MEDAL FOR HORSEMANSHIP AT THE 1932 OLYMPICS IN LOS ANGELES. HE OWNED EXOTIC SPORTS CARS.

HE SOCIALIZED WITH HOLLYWOOD STARS AND WORE DESIGNER CLOTHES.

IT TOOK UNTIL THE NEXT DAY WHEN THE REMAINS OF CUSHMAN'S BATTALION COULD WITHDRAW UNDER COVERING FIRE FROM U.S. TANKS.

FIGHTING CONTINUED IN THAT AREA AND IT BECAME KNOWN AS "CUSHMAN'S POCKET."

ON THE NIGHT OF D+16, JAPA-
NESE NAVY CAPTAIN INOUYE LED
A BANZAI ATTACK ON THE
AIRFIELDS.

HE HAD DISOBEYED GENERAL
KURIBAYASHI'S ORDERS.

THE MARINES FIRED FLARES AND
STAR SHELLS THAT LIT UP THE
BATTLEFIELD AS IF IT WERE BROAD
DAYLIGHT.

THE CHARGE WAS MET HEAD-ON
WITH FIRE FROM MARINE
MACHINE GUNS, RIFLES, AND
MORTARS.

THE MORNING LIGHT REVEALED MORE
THAN 800 JAPANESE DEAD.

LT. JACK LUMMUS WAS A FORMER ROOKIE END FOR THE NEW YORK GIANTS FOOTBALL TEAM.

ON MARCH 8, 1945 (D+17) HE WAS LEADING HIS PLATOON IN THE PUSH NORTH TOWARD KITANO POINT.

DESPITE HAVING BEEN KNOCKED DOWN TWICE BY ENEMY GRENADES, LT. LUMMUS SINGLE-HANDEDLY ATTACKED AND SILENCED TWO PILLBOXES.

AS HE WAS RUNNING AHEAD OF HIS MEN, URGING THEM FORWARD, LUMMUS STEPPED ON A MINE. IT BLEW OFF BOTH HIS LEGS.

WHEN THE SMOKE CLEARED LUMMUS WAS STANDING ON HIS STUMPS, WAVING ON HIS MEN.

DON'T STOP NOW, KEEP GOING!

LT. LUMMUS DIED THAT AFTER-NOON IN A FIELD HOSPITAL.

ON THE NIGHT OF MARCH 9 (D+18) MARINES SETTLING DOWN AFTER ANOTHER DAY OF FIERCE FIGHTING WERE CHEERED TO HEAR A TREMENDOUS ROARING SOUND TO THE EAST.

B-29S -- HEADING NORTH!

HUNDREDS OF THEM!

IT WAS THE FIRST OF GENERAL CURTIS LEMAY'S FIREBOMBING RAIDS ON TOKYO.

THERE WERE 325 B-29S FROM GUAM, TINIAN, AND SAIPAN.

IN THAT ONE NIGHT, A QUARTER OF TOKYO WAS DESTROYED AND 83,793 PEOPLE (MOSTLY CIVILIANS) WERE KILLED.

BY MARCH 10, D+19, GENERAL KURIBAYASHI WAS DOWN TO 1,500 MEN. HE PREPARED TO MAKE HIS LAST STAND IN THE CRAGGY NORTH-WEST CORNER OF THE ISLAND. IT WOULD COME TO BE KNOWN AS "DEATH VALLEY."

IN CUSHMAN'S POCKET, THE MARINE 3RD DIVISION FINISHED OFF THE REMAINS OF BARON NISHI'S TANK REGIMENT.

FLAMETHROWER TANKS HAD USED 10,000 GALLONS OF FUEL EACH DAY.

BARON NISHI AND HIS STAFF FOUGHT TO THE END FROM A MAZE OF CAVES AND TUNNELS.

HIS BODY WAS NEVER RECOVERED.

IN AN AREA BETWEEN AIRFIELD 2 AND THE SEA, SEABEES, AIR FORCE PERSONNEL, AND SHORE PARTIES WERE ASLEEP DURING THE DARK EARLY MORNING HOURS.

THEY WERE SURE THAT THE FIGHTING WAS ALMOST OVER.

BUT 300 JAPANESE SOLDIERS FROM DEATH VALLEY CHARGED INTO THE CAMP AND CAUGHT EVERYONE BY SURPRISE.

MEN WERE BAYONETED IN THEIR SLEEP.

FIGHTING STARTED OUT AT CLOSE RANGE WITH GRENADES AND PISTOLS.

THE FIGHT THEN BECAME A DESPERATE HAND-TO-HAND COMBAT IN PITCH DARKNESS.

MARINES FROM THE PIONEER BATTALION AND TROOPS FROM THE SHORE PARTY JOINED THE BATTLE, SHOOTING, KICKING, AND STABBING.

IN THE MORNING, 44 AIRMEN AND 9 MARINES LAY DEAD. THERE WERE 119 AMERICAN WOUNDED.

JAPANESE LOSSES WERE 262 KILLED AND 18 CAPTURED.

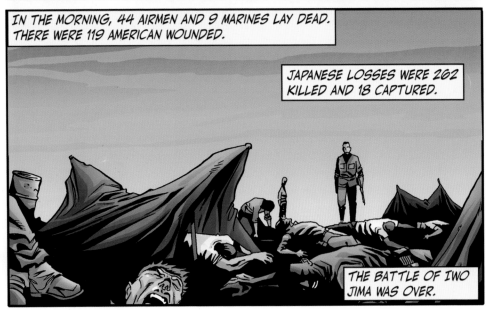

THE BATTLE OF IWO JIMA WAS OVER.

NOBODY KNOWS WHAT HAPPENED TO GENERAL KURIBAYASHI. IF HE WAS KILLED AND BURIED ON IWO JIMA, THE LOCATION OF HIS GRAVE IS A MYSTERY.

GENERAL HOLLAND SMITH SPENT A WHOLE DAY SEARCHING FOR KURIBAYASHI'S BODY IN ORDER TO GIVE HIM A PROPER BURIAL.

HE SAID OF KURIBAYASHI, "HE WAS OUR MOST REDOUBTABLE ADVERSARY."

OF THE MORE THAN 21,000 JAPANESE TROOPS WHO DEFENDED IWO JIMA, ONLY 1,083 SURVIVED TO BE TAKEN PRISONER.

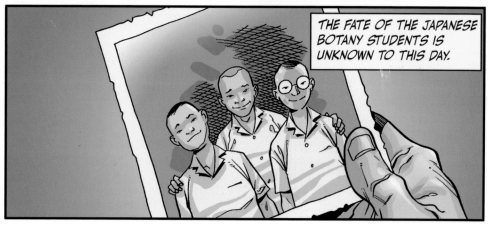

THE FATE OF THE JAPANESE BOTANY STUDENTS IS UNKNOWN TO THIS DAY.

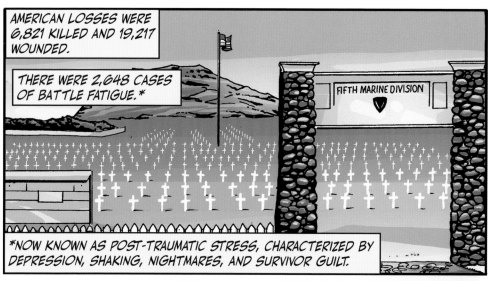

AMERICAN LOSSES WERE 6,821 KILLED AND 19,217 WOUNDED.

THERE WERE 2,648 CASES OF BATTLE FATIGUE.*

FIFTH MARINE DIVISION

*NOW KNOWN AS POST-TRAUMATIC STRESS, CHARACTERIZED BY DEPRESSION, SHAKING, NIGHTMARES, AND SURVIVOR GUILT.

27 CONGRESSIONAL MEDALS OF HONOR WERE AWARDED FOR ACTS OF UNDENIABLE HEROISM ON IWO JIMA.

DOUGLAS JACOBSON, GEORGE WAHLEN, AND HERSHEL WILLIAMS WERE AMONG THE LIVING RECIPIENTS OF THE MEDAL.

DARREN COLE AND JACK LUMMUS RECEIVED POSTHUMOUS AWARDS.

ON AUGUST 6, 1945, THE B-29 *ENOLA GAY* DROPPED THE FIRST ATOMIC BOMB ON HIROSHIMA.

AFTER A SECOND NUCLEAR WEAPON WAS DROPPED ON NAGASAKI, JAPAN SURRENDERED.

COLONEL PAUL TIBBETS, WHO PILOTED THE *ENOLA GAY*, SAID, "MORE THAN 2,220 AIRCRAFT MADE EMERGENCY LANDINGS ON IWO."

"HAD IT NOT BEEN FOR THE HEROIC VALOR OF THE MARINES IN SECURING THE ISLAND AND THE SEABEES IN BUILDING THE RUNWAYS, MORE THAN 22,000 PILOTS AND AIRCREW WOULD HAVE PERISHED IN CRASH LANDINGS IN THE SEA."

AT THE DEDICATION OF THE MARINE CORPS MEMORIAL AT ARLINGTON NATIONAL CEMETERY, ARLINGTON, VIRGINIA, GENERAL HOLLAND SMITH WAS SEATED IN THE LAST ROW OF THE BLEACHERS.

ENGRAVED ON THE MONUMENT IS ADMIRAL CHESTER NIMITZ'S TRIBUTE TO THE MARINES OF IWO JIMA: "UNCOMMON VALOR WAS A COMMON VIRTUE."

IRA HAYES RETURNED TO ARIZONA OVERWHELMED BY SURVIVOR GUILT AND IGNORED BY HIS OWN TRIBE.

HE SPENT TWO YEARS, THIRTY DAYS AT A TIME, IN THE PHOENIX JAIL FOR DRUNKENNESS, WHERE THEY LET HIM RAISE THE FLAG EVERY MORNING.

AFTER A NIGHT OF DRINKING, HE PASSED OUT FACEDOWN IN A CANAL AND DROWNED IN THREE INCHES OF WATER.

A PHOENIX POLICEMAN WHO OFTEN ARRESTED HAYES SAID, "HE WAS A HERO TO EVERYBODY BUT HIMSELF."

ON JANUARY 8, 2004, THE SALT LAKE UTAH VETERANS AFFAIRS MEDICAL CENTER WAS RENAMED TO HONOR GEORGE E. WAHLEN.

GEORGE E. WAHLEN
MEDICAL CENTER

IN 1945, WHEN WAHLEN WAS AWARDED THE MEDAL OF HONOR, A REPORTER ASKED HIM HOW HE EARNED IT. WAHLEN REPLIED SIMPLY, "I CONTINUED TO TAKE CARE OF CASUALTIES WHEN I WAS WOUNDED."

THE END

COUNTDOWN TO TOTAL VICTORY

On the night of March 9–10, 1945, General LeMay's B-29 Superfortresses carried out a new method of air attack against the Japanese. Most of the plane's guns were removed, and the bombers were armed with firebombs. Using Iwo Jima, now in American control, as a navigation marker, they attacked Tokyo at night. The fires burned out of control, and the city became a furnace of death and destruction. In the days that followed, Nagoya, Kobe, and Osaka were hit. In ten days, the Superfortresses flattened 32 square miles of Japan's most important centers.

The Japanese military was worried about their chances for a glorious final battle. By June 1945, B-29s started bombing Japan during the day, escorted by fighters from Iwo Jima. Japan was now being hit day and night by the giant Superfortress bombers. Japanese fighter planes were driven from the sky. Soon many vital Japanese industries and factories were destroyed, such as aircraft engine and oil production manufacturers.

Meanwhile, a photograph of U.S. soldiers raising the American flag at Iwo Jima had energized Americans at home. Its heroic image, together with American losses at the tiny island—almost 21,000 casualties, including almost 7,000 dead—proudly reminded Americans of the important struggle the nation was involved in.

General Kuribayashi had succeeded in his main purpose at Iwo Jima. By inflicting heavy casualties on the Americans, he showed what the Allies could expect in an invasion of Japan. The Americans estimated that the invasion of Japan, scheduled for November 1, 1945, would cost an estimated one million casualties and at least two million Japanese. To many people in the U.S. government and military, such terrible loss of life could be risked only as a last resort. However, as history

Cameraman Joe Rosenthal took the most famous photograph of World War II with this picture of six Marines raising the flag on Mount Suribachi, Iwo Jima, February 23, 1945.

shows, the United States did have another option in its effort to totally defeat the Japanese. As early as 1942, work had secretly begun on developing a nuclear bomb. By July 1945 such a bomb was ready to be tested—although not even the people who worked on it were sure it would work. But the tests were successful, and on August 6 a nuclear bomb was dropped on the Japanese city of Hiroshima. Three days later, another bomb was dropped on Nagasaki. Three days later, the Japanese surrendered. Both bombs were dropped by Boeing B-29s.

adversary An opponent or enemy.

amphibious Launched from the sea against an enemy on land.

artillery Large, heavy guns that are mounted on wheels or tracks.

ball bearing A bearing in which the moving and stationary parts are held apart by small steel balls that turn in a collar around the moving parts and reduce friction.

barrage A heavy outpouring of many things at once.

blockhouse A fortification made of concrete with slits for firing or observation.

bombardment An attack of bombs, shells, or other explosives.

botany The scientific study of plants.

compressed Pressed together; made smaller by pressure.

diplomat A person who has been appointed to represent a government in its dealing with other governments.

disabled Inoperative.

elder An older influential person of a family, tribe, or community.

emplacement A prepared position for heavy guns.

entrust To turn over to another for safekeeping, care, or action.

evacuate To send away or withdraw from an area.

extend To enlarge the area, scope, or range of.

fortifications Military works erected to fortify a position or place.

inflict To cause pain or suffering.

materiel Equipment and supplies.

mortar A cannon used to fire shells in a high arc.

pillbox A small concrete structure for a machine gun or other weapon.

platoon A unit of soldiers smaller than a company but larger than a squad, normally commanded by a lieutenant.

posthumous Occurring after one's death.

preceding Existing or coming before another or others in time, place, rank, or sequence.

redoubtable Worthy of respect or honor.

regiment A unit of troops made up of two or more battalions.

reservist A member of a military reserve.

sniper A person who shoots at others from a hiding place.

summit The highest point or part; the top, especially of a mountain.

sway To have influence on or control over.

taboo A ban or an inhibition resulting from social custom or tradition.

tactical Of, relating to, or using the military science of moving and directing troops, ships, and aircraft against an enemy.

terrace A raised bank of earth having vertical or sloping sides and a flat top.

ORGANIZATIONS

Iwo Jima Monument and Memorial Museum
320 Iwo Jima Boulevard
Harlingen, TX 78550
(956) 412-2207
Web site: http://www.mma-tx.org/museum.htm

National Museum of the Marine Corps
Quantico, VA 22134
(703) 432-4877
Web site: http://www.usmcmuseum.org/Programs_museum.asp

FOR FURTHER READING

Black, Wallace B., and Jean F. Blashfield. *Iwo Jima and Okinawa.* Englewood Cliffs, NJ: Silver Burdett Press, 1992.

Dorr, Robert. *B-29 Units of World War II.* Oxford, England: Osprey Publishing, 2002.

Ienaga, Saburo. *Pacific War, 1931–1945.* News York: Pantheon Books, 1979.

Marling, Karal Ann, and John Wetenhall. *Iwo Jima: Moments, Memories and the American Hero.* Cambridge, MA: Harvard University Press, 1991.

Wright, Derrick. *Iwo Jima 1945: The Marines Raise the Flag on Mount Suribachi.* Oxford, England: Osprey Publishing, 2001.

INDEX

A
adversary, 40
amphibious, 8–9, 11
artillery, 6, 10, 14, 22, 27, 30–31

B
ball bearing, 12
banzai charge, 7, 33
barrage, 31
blockhouse, 16–17, 26
Boeing B-29 Superfortress bomber, 4–5, 12, 22, 30, 35, 42, 44–45
bombardment, 7, 10
botany, 16, 40

C
carriers, 8, 18, 31
caves, 7, 15, 36
compressed, 24

D
diplomat, 13
disabled, 10

E
elder, 21
emplacement, 15, 24, 26
entrust, 11
evacuate, 23
extend, 22

F
fortifications, 15

H
Hayes, Ira, 21, 43
Higashikuni, Prince and Commander of Home Defense Headquarters, 5
Hirohito, Emperor, 3, 5

I
inflict, 15

K
kamikaze attacks, 7, 18
Kuribayashi, Lt. General Tadamichi, 3, 6–7, 13, 15, 29, 33, 36–37, 40, 44

L
landing craft, 7, 9–10

M
Marianas Islands, 4–7, 12
marines, 7–11, 17–21, 23–29, 31, 33, 35–36, 39, 42
materiel, 4
minefields, 7, 26, 34
mortar, 33
Mt. Suribachi, 19–20

N
Nimitz, Admiral Chester, 11, 42
Nishi, Lt. Colonel Baron Taeichi, 3, 32, 36

P
pillbox, 7, 15, 17, 34
platoon, 34
posthumous, 41
preceding, 10

R
radar warning station, 5, 12
redoubtable, 40
regiment, 17, 20, 24, 32, 36
reservist, 26
Rosenthal, Joe, 21

S
Schmidt, Major General Harry "The Dutchman," 7, 11, 22
Smith, General Holland M. "Howling Mad," 3, 6, 11, 19, 29, 40, 42
sniper, 22
Spruance, Admiral Raymond, 3, 5, 7, 11
summit, 19–20
sway, 37

T
taboo, 21
tactical, 6–7, 11
tanks, 9, 14, 25, 27, 31–32, 36
terrace, 9, 14, 17
Tojo, Prime Minister Hideki, 5
tunnels, 7, 15, 36

WEB SITES

Due to the changing nature of Internet links, the Rosen Publishing Group, Inc., has developed an online list of Web sites related to the subject of this book. This site is updated regularly. Please use this link to access the list:

http://www.rosenlinks.com/gbww2/ij